Bistro

KATE NORTH

Published by Cinnamon Press
Meirion House, Glan yr afon, Tanygrisiau
Blaenau Ffestiniog, Gwynedd, LL41 3SU
www.cinnamonpress.com
The right of Kate North to be identified as author of this work has been asserted by her in accordance with the Copyright, Designs and Patent Act, 1988.
ISBN: 978-1-907090-73-8

British Library Cataloguing in Publication Data. A CIP record for this book can be obtained from the British Library.

Designed and typeset in Palatino by Cinnamon Press
Cover from original artwork 'Menu' by Micheli Sola & 'Bistro' by Benjamin Haas' © Agency: dreamstime.com
Cover design by Jan Fortune

Printed in Poland

Cinnamon Press is represented in the UK by Inpress Ltd www.inpressbooks.co.uk and in Wales by the Welsh Books Council www.cllc.org.uk

The publisher gratefully acknowledges the support of the Welsh Books Council

Kate North grew up in Cardiff where she now lives and teaches. She has an MA in Creative Writing from the University of East Anglia and a PhD in Creative and Critical Writing from Cardiff University. Kate currently edits for *Iota Magazine*.
Her first novel was *Eva Shell* (Cinnamon, 2008).

Acknowledgments

Some of these poems have appeared previously in *Poetry Wales*, *Orbis* and *Scintilla*. Further poems have been published in the anthologies *Magpie* (UEA, 2000), *Reactions* (Pen&ink, 2000), *The Pterodactyl's Wing* (Parthian, 2003), *This Line is Not for Turning* (Cinnamon, 2011) and *Not a Muse* (Haven, 2009).

I would like to thank Alex for her unwavering support and confidence in me.

Contents

Sunbathing in Llangrannog

Bistro

The Birth of Venus

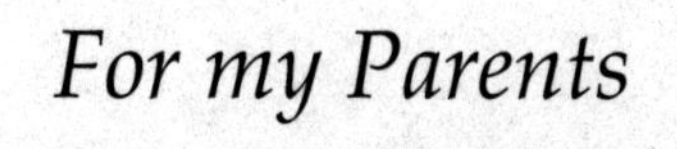

For my Parents

Sunbathing in Llangrannog

Eight

I

This is years ago
and I'm waiting in my room.
I'm sitting on my bed
with my back to the door.

As I stare at the corkboard wall
it looks like marble
and veins and a London Underground map.
It's a riverbed deposit as well.

Thump thump, thump thump, thump thump,
(*staircase*)
Thump,
(*landing stair*)
Bang, Crash,
(*door against desk*)

My mother's voice precedes
the parting of her lips.
I've got the screenplay in my brain.
We're both flying in the eye of the tornado.
We're clicking our shoes.
and when she lands
my mother throws over my bookcase
onto the floor.

II

Ten minutes have passed,
So, it's safe to view the wreckage.
I can't see any breakages
as I begin the salvage operation.

I can smell the Mr Sheen
hovering in her space.
It's a Sunday.

On this day of worship,
and other scary times,
I find an aged box.

The edges of the lid are torn,
the pattern is of purple and gold.
Inside is a family book,
the book in the box lives under my bed.
I look at it as if I've never seen it before.
I take off the lid in archaeologist mode.

I'm also blocking away the sound
of slamming cutlery drawers downstairs.

Painting for the Nodes

for J.N.

It's a hot one
today
when I call
and you sound relieved
picking up.

Thanks
you declare
before even asking;
it's obvious
I will,
we all will.

I arrive
at yours alive
and ask.
You show me
to the spare room.

Walls and skirting,
if it's not too much.
Stop
when you've had enough,
you say.

And you disappear
downstairs
to the floorboards.
The house is full
of helpers
useful and useless.

I make my way
with rollers,
paint.
This is my first
brush with emulsion.

Your spare room
is a suntrap
in the afternoons.
I stand, hoping
in a glare of light,
that this will make a difference.

Earlier
our Mother told me
in confidence
that she wanted
to place her hand on your neck
claw inside
pull out the decay
place it in her mouth
and swallow.
When you come to check,
to declare my skill and diligence,
parade your happiness,
my gaze flickers
between yours
and the neck.
It is getting bigger
and I revert
to kneeling and smoothing the gloss
on the skirting.

Left alone
I decide to tackle the door.
Not on your list
but obviously required.
As I daub at wood panels
sweat merges with tear
high on my cheek.
I annoy myself with the inappropriate,
memories that prove
we don't always get along.

And now I'm left
painting
offering lifts
making calls of concern
reading up
having late night chats
with all those people
who have come out to care;
for what it's worth.

Icarus the Kite Flyer

From the window your bright fabric directs my eyes
in looping motions erratic
as the wind causing your dream-on-a-string to pull.

Taut arms upwards
open mouth suggesting
the world's pigeons beating in your chest.

I want to curve through the air
reaching for your colours
cling onto a ride that's not mine.

Sunbathing in Llangrannog

I can see me dipping my toes over the side of a squeaky, air bloated mat. Arms flapping in and out now, annoying myself, directing the spray onto my lenses. The Sun burns through the water through the glass through my eyes.

…now rain shoots up from the Earth's core like little tinsel rockets, clouds frown like crabs stranded on a shoreline, rabbits carry Spanish acrobats on their backs…

I can see you sat, a diver mid tuck, rocking back and forth like an unstable Polar Bear. Opening each sandwich before you eat, checking for rogue ingredients. Then you spill the egg mayonnaise down your chin, quickly you wipe away the evidence and check that no one else has seen.

Advice on Heavy Petting in Coastal Areas

Have yourself a healthy serving
of pie and chips and gravy
then splash it over your face.
Smear it across your torso
in brown and lumpy smudges.

Get a close friend
to lick at you, like a platter
of delicate veal served cold
and fresh in the afternoon's air.

Make sure this is done in public
on a bandstand in a park,
on a pier or an esplanade.

But – don't stick your tongue
down anybody's throat,
not even as an hors d'oeuvre.
It's bad manners.

Postcard I Didn't Like to Send

I am now in the valley for the summer
and await your arrival.
I write this from the boulder we pushed
near the rockery last year,
in order to catch the breeze for writing.

I am looking to the cottage,
with shutters in need of paint,
the insect screen is torn.
The door hangs lower than before, forced.

The dogs lie on the porch
like hardened-black beef
warped in the heat and infested
with yellow movement in their bullet holes.

Inside, the cocktail bar has been disgraced
to shards scattering through the lounge
and about the house in glints.

There is no
light nor food nor sound,
only a stench that the lavender patch
cannot compete with.

The bathroom is fouled
and the linoleum is now dangerous
with mud and crap.
I have spent the morning
scrubbing lipstick graffiti from our walls.

The weather is still
the neighbours are away.

Tantrum

Not a comet this one,
nothing like it,
without build up and international recognition;
not a comet.

A different type of missile
like a baseball. In its way
a canary playing chase with a rocket.

Without breaks
it doesn't stop to think itself
a Kamikaze pilot rattling into oblivion.

Like an indignant teenager
crossing that line,
swimming right through
not around the buoy.

Fizzing like a sundae
through thick frosted glass,
then gone – nothing left to make it real.

The Man With Two Left Feet

for M.O.

I'll take you dancing.

Please, not dancing.
How I long to waltz
my arm locked across your waist.
Crossing realms reserved for brothers,
sharing pulses designed for lovers.
Each foot placed by my desire for your melody
that toys with my spin.
Getting to hold you like I shouldn't,
grappling with your taffeta wings.

When You Ended It…

We were walking across the rugby pitch
short-cut home.
The try posts framed a cloaca bound sun
as you cupped my face
with your disinfected hands.

Your mouth decomposed into a compost smile,
my cheeks blistered with red disturbance.
Then, at the try line
your curtain call tongue spoke.

Look, there's a magpie –
let's salute him.
I don't believe in such games
and it happened to be a peacock.

Bistro

Bistro

Behind the vibrant ink spots
that bubble around her,
sat in immediate distance
like a beetle over her plate,
at the smallest table
cramped on the bistro's smallest chair
the shy lunch eater picks at a meal
bigger than her face.

Jabbing her cutlery like chopsticks
into a Mediterranean work of art,
the waiter coughs
a disguised glance as he passes.

Reaching for the teapot
inspecting its bowels before she proceeds
to draw her drink in a long and elegant hand;
the woman looks taller for her efforts.

She's twitching each muscle in her neck
alternately, showing signs
that she's experiencing the new, alone.

This visitor crept into her unfamiliar,
my familiar space.
Not without permission
but with worry and eager witness.

Now she picks and inspects
like she's feeling that she shouldn't,
and is careful to place the napkin
as she found it, at the end of the meal.

Acts of

Contrition 1979

Oh my God, thank you for loving me.
I am sorry for all my sins,
for not loving others and not loving you.
Help me to live like Jesus, and not sin again.
Amen.

Contrition 1989

Oh my God, thank you for shoving me.
I am sorry for all my songs,
for not living others and not living you.
Help me to love like Jesus, and not sing again
Amen.

Cognition 1998

Oh my Word, thank you for showing me.
I am sorry for all my wrongs,
for not knowing others and not knowing you.
Help me to live again
Amen.

Coition 2001

Oh my love, thank you for moving me.
I am happy for all our strength,
for not knowing others and now knowing you.
Help me to live like an Aeolian, so we can sing again.
Amen.

Detrition 2009

Oh my eye, thank you for loving me,
I am scared for all these things;
for not knowing where I am, or with whom.
Help me to live through this
then never again.

Fantasising Herself

She looks to the desert mirror
and sees a woman curling around the dunes tonight.

Lost on the slopes,
she sits and slides downwards,
landing where the sand begins to ripple.

The dry pond smoothes through her skin
raffias her neck, arms, ankles, head.

She sculpts a tent with vigour
then rests. On her back

she views the glass slivers
in between their blinking,
embedded in the roof of her world.

I Clicked

I clicked my fingers once and ordered a book,
from the thick briny air around me. When my click
was heard the word was sent, in tea for protection
and the environment's sake.

On hands and knees I sift, fanning my arms ahead
into the loose misty tea scattered over planks of floor.
Cutting a trench, I pile leaves to the left and right of me.
I am looking for something in this, something to...
how you say...Logos? To read? A book? Something
to read in the leaves.

Before I can read the leaves I've ordered, I must read
the leaves that encase them. This is where I find
such things as contradictions, baggage.
It would be the same if I took tobacco, leaves wrapped
in a thinner, paler leaf holding all together.

But this isn't just about the unification of leaves. It's also
about dismissal, the sour leaves that I won't take.
I know one has to taste a leaf first before it turns sour.
Which came first, the tobacco or the thé?

I'm told both were from colonies, and before that,
from tribes, before that, the ground, a swamp, the sea.
This is how such delicacies have been brought to me.

I am told that I am of a colony, a tribe, the ground,
a swamp, the sea. Read this in my clannish flesh,
in the grooves of my identity, my crying gaelic eyes
that rotate in their dark greek sockets, my webbed
welsh feet. I am the english.

Bankers

We wear cotton
crushed by the flat heat, or the iron,
and slacks that starch our female figures.

Row, desk
paper, woman.
Out slip
in slip.

Our wrists flick through the credits
and hotly at the keys, we finger numerals
with manicure precision.

A gaggle of whores
legs spread, for numbers
sheer in amount.

Last spring we made confetti
in the *bureau de change,* from old currency,
then hid it in the strong room
beneath a crate of cheques.

A harem of nurses
dressed in and dressing
an infected wound.

Once, a manager in royal blue chintz
spat a visit on our in-trays.
It landed, curling the papers below,
upwards as they yellowed.

A doe-eyed bunch
an underclass, spoken to in doggerel,
useless.

Thirty times smaller than I

Jesus' gilt torso is flung in a child's playful leap,
his legs bend impatiently
against a decorated crucifix,
waxen toes drip from his limbs
to collect at the base.

Code continually shifts
dispersing to some other place,
there are toes and tears
crosses and cakes
thorns and beds,
words that won't glue to a page.

A man no bigger than my palm is bleeding.
Eight pints of blood in the human body
$\div 30 = 0.26^{r}$
The silver saviour on my wall is bleeding
0.26 pints for us
recurring, recurring, recurring

On Being European

I

He has a speech phobia
and is not to blame.

Embarrassing to watch
people frustrated by him
when it's obvious they just want
to stuff an oiled rag in his mouth
to loosen up his jaw.

As a baby he wailed – cried the walls away,
waaah, waaah, waaah,
hideous all the time. Nervous parents
and eggshell carpets.

Then he slipped from a wall,
over and over with various landings,
sweet.

No voice after that. Pity and bless, as they say.
Just sits now, a stationary exile,
even statues usually speak a little.

II

Do you think his chair has wrists?
Feel its pulse through the upholstery then
when you cross your legs over it, catch your garments
on the rough of its wicker.

And by pulse I don't mean rings,
counting them when you're nine
to find out that the tree is twelve like your brother
or thirty three like poor Aunt Jane.

Pulse like the dovetail of its join
and the scuff of its shin. Like the stain of its polish,
a happy lament.

Couch potatoes the lot of us:
A continent of slackers
firing odds and shouting blanks. *Comedia.*
Non arte.

Like the jerk of a writer
who sat in front of the mirror
a welcome distraction from the page, necessary.
If you can't look yourself in the eye then who else can?

Backwards narrative sold well for a while.

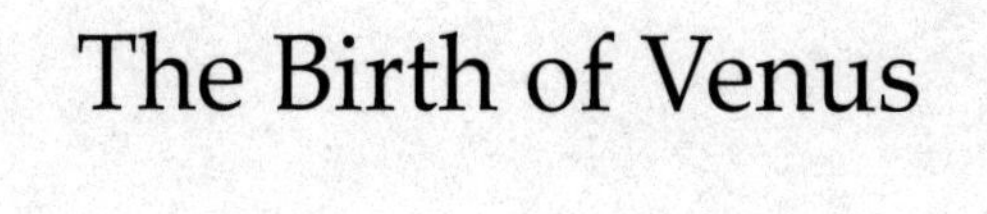

The Birth of Venus

The Birth of Venus

A dart is flying down the M4 this evening.
When she hits home
she'll take the wind out of everyone's sails.
But as she's stripping off, she's growing.

With a smile like a canoe that's announcing,
all sorts of baggage resting in the boot,
she walks through the front door and declares;

I'm growing my hair.
I'm heading to Llangrannog.
I'm going to that little cave where I sat with you.
I'll count all the pearls of the coast,
trying to keep them here
in my lap.

Today I made myself a necklace of pearls.
Significant rounds, sea sliding across my neck.
Give me more for my arms and legs,
let them be painted,
I want to glow in the dark.

Sleep Disorder

This is the second night
I find myself staring at your face
remembering who you are.
One of your earrings is missing
and I freeze with the knowledge
that you wear them, obliged to store the fact
in case I need a gift idea.

Still staring, through your features,
I compose speeches in advance for the lover
the estranged, the corrupt, the beautiful.
Sometimes braving a line aloud to be
repeated with various inflection,
ready for the day I will use it.

Unmoved by noises in the building;
a background of loved ones
with loved ones arriving and passing
through the otherwise static of my mind,
I conduct a tour of your shadow
stopping at alien places
whilst searching for the familiar.
Panic ensues when I see that yours
could be any leg,
and what is ours about the embryo curve
of your body as you sleep?
Mine are the shirt you wear and the mules kicked to freedom,
now conspiring from the floor.
That is all. And I try not to stare at these
because they lurk in a half light near the door,
looking as sprightly as I did
several hours ago, leaving in a taxi.

The extra day I give myself in this bed
is not shared with you.
The contented hum of breath is yours
but I play with it inches away, mimicking the beat
of your hiss in my own way,
for comparison. I do not feel I know
what it is to be you asleep, and breathing.

I lie next to the edge of the bed and wonder
if you mind being by the wall.
I would mind having to stretch over me
to reach the water jug
in the middle of the night.
I would mind waking to the stare
of angry plasterboard.
I would mind not having access to the lamp.

As my game grows bigger I cannot help consulting
the rule, the one rule that is; you must not wake.
Each turn must not break the rule,
so I slow down. Then I aim for the ceiling with my eyes,
there is nothing up there
except the wallpaper that belongs on the wall,
not the ceiling.
There is no fun here,
only the beginnings of a sleep
that starts to take shape
as I begin to relent.

This is interrupted by you
who I was so careful not to disturb.
Your jealous arm thrashes a wide semi-circle
through the air as you roll towards me,
then it lands across my chest
a seatbelt keeping me flat and awake.
This is your *lover's arm,*
the liberation you feel in protecting my body
while you sleep is your reward.

I know you want to wake like this, in a while,
wake finding your limbs wrapped around me,
because they may do as they please
in the dark, unfelt and unseen by you.
You hope they will become a surprise
by morning.

I want to lift your arm
like the raising of a bridge
and slide from underneath as a surreal clock,
off the bed and onto the floor.
Then you will wake and neither of us will sleep
and the time I am having will be gone.
I cannot brave it.

I am as still as a girder
supporting our connection.
At first I feel like a bell-hop
opening doors for guests,
then uncomfortable as well as polite.
I am allowing your treat, protecting
your comfort from my movement
and the fact that my eyes are open
buzzing in every direction,
due to the wires in my brain
that sizzle without rest.
I am helping your elderly and frail body
across the road, guilty
that I recognise your inability
to sense danger in oncoming traffic.

You are moving across me and then back
as soon as your momentum wanes.
I am Kilimanjaro.
I do not move as your arm slackens
around me like a flag against its pole in still air
which does nothing to ease
the drying of my mouth.
My habits breed failure when
I realise that I too will not reach
the water jug, for fear of unsettling you.

I resign myself to the practical.
When you wake I will pamper you
like I pamper myself on a Sunday morning.
I will urge you to sleep a little more,
until I return with your mediocre newspaper
your choice of breakfast,
and my own dumbed down indulgences.
I can manage to replace
my bagel with your croissants,
sure that our tastes will reunite
in coffee over tea.
I will buy painkillers at the shop
so that when tiredness mutates into an ache,
I will be at ease, having taken one more
than prescribed on the short walk back.
The new invigorated me you see
will be the same as the girl yesterday morning.
You don't notice my reinvention in your sleep.

Reaching a lazy stage causes my neck to relax
so that our noses nearly meet.
I can smell your skin from here,
I can see the complicated pores
that look like minute and bashful sewer grids,
paving the waste that runs beneath
your epidermis. I am entranced
by this maze of ducts that coat your surface
as if paisley or herring bone.
This is your tweed
that does not make me itch.
Later today I want you to patent your design,
so no one else may wear it.
Then I will patent my right,
so no one else will see your fabric.

I am compelled to watch
the sculpture of your skin,
I fear my vocabulary will suffer
if I allow my eyes to leave.

I am caught in your face when your eyes open.
You make no exclamation,
no words or movement seep into the occasion.
I am staring and am caught in the act
of betrayal. All that has gone before
is out with my intrigued eyes.
You see you are in bed with a madwoman –
a foaming dog who should know better.
You may leave if you wish, but do not.
You sleep again and I continue
as planned, returning to read and eat with you.

I sit upright in our bed and remember
the periods of calm,
the bouts of sheet twisting,
my cautious writhing through the dark.
You nurse my head with soft strokes
and invoke a silence
that no longer contains a sleeper beside me.

High Tea

We sit on stone,
an ancient table now daubed with check.
Our cellophane wrappings
wing through the tussle of our feet
and the grass.

It's amusing to discuss the past
when we're in it. This could be
where the druids came
with mistletoe, so I kiss you.

There were martyrs once,
strapped down then left
un-flinching.

The perfect place
for an offering – lamb split
sliced down its whole and spilling
over the lip of a carved boulder.

It could have had something to do with babies,
rocks set in the round
for healthy generations to come.

Now it is so still
and general in its shape;
the puzzle puts us in full focus.

Twenty Minutes on the London Eye

This is a fantasy

The city is about me
when you are on me with your lunar smile
and gossipy calves,
we revolve through our ordeal
a display.

We trip the commuter's gaze like always
on the morning skyline
and feign embarrassment only after we have finished.

This is a present

A sentimental ride
blossoming angles of skin
into, through and out of ourselves.

White coin in the clouds
jaunty as a cartwheel unbound
from her carriage.

This is a day trip

Lying with Croeso I

I am taking you out
and you are wearing language
like a dress. This is how you will talk
to me tonight.

You look like you can sing
and do so, as we travel over a border
to a recommended chef near an estuary.

Our palates chatter.

After coffee you talk me through your skirts,
folds of garnish over pale limbs,
tucked away limbs.
I am a moth plucking at threads.

I place myself carefully and we share
no words, only their beginnings.

Quits it's Doubles

As outfits go, yours is gone
along with shirts and slippers
camisole and watch.

I still own the half-items,
those utility items
you never understood,
or put to use.

I'm on the lino, back resting
in the grooves of a cupboard door
varnished last Christmas.

You wanted it done before
they came, I remember a midnight mass
of chemical incense anointing the kitchen,
blessing the turkey.

Did we make the bed
or just put it together
racking those slats like a spine,
strong backbone to the start of the stars?

We made it but you designed it.
A cavern beneath us for storage of nephews, sheets, shoes.

I'm on the lino
blade in groove and spinning
empty tumbler under hand
as I stare ahead to the whorl,
a washing machine that looks like static.

Of course, there is not the need to wash as before,
you have taken your shirts and camisole.

I can roll across the frontiers of the duvet and into your county,
dirty it up and down before I need to peel away the layers
and let them soak.

Written for the Only Woman

The only woman that I have always known,
she loves me like this.

She kept me in a fortress,
no, a tower.
I had long blonde hair,
I had a big white horse, of course.

She dined me like a queen every night,
on quince and toast;
My only maid ladling my milk
into champagne flutes,
then I'd sprinkle chocolate drops on the top.

Now I'm gnawing at my limbs,
something that I can't stop.

The only woman,
what does she see?
A girl who can't stop
because she tastes so good.

The Snow Spits

The snow spits into the porch and onto my wrists. I clutch at your remote voice and whisper surfacing thoughts into the thick espresso view. We are not on the phone, we are downstairs awake, staying up late for the third night in a row, like mothers on the cusp of delivery. The house creaks as I inhale.

Okay?
Okay?

Next door's Tom tiptoes past a refracting beam, a grumbling door or, a saddened window anticipating its use as a hollow moon dips into the frame, lowers her lids but doesn't let them shut.

Through the cracks private words string by then pop as though balloons. Down shrivels the casing onto the ledge and up flies helium.

Lying with Croeso II

You took me out
in silence, with a bare back
and dipping neckline, clicking your heels
to my face for conversation.

You stared through the windscreen
all way there, tunnelling through
the night to a lake I'd never heard of.

We ate there, excitedly.

I spoke about breath,
friction, and the shapes that lips make
pronouncing vowels. You nodded.

I placed myself carefully
and we shared words but no beginnings.

Shoe

All that was left when they took a boy
away from the lush pasture filled
with choirs of children catching the ears
of the vigilant for blocks around.

Worn at the heel and curled at the toe,
not even whole. Gashes through
blue-brown leather, slaver and tooth-score
on the tongue.

Next to the burst ball
in an area of ground down grass
blades still falling and collecting in clumps.

Buckled, an impossible shape
sunning its sole in front of a crowd
mumbling and cursing around the object.

The item that survived
to testify, a remark
made by a mad dog, a statement
left on the green.

Jury Service

Taking a swig she let it loll in her mouth as if it were part of a sacred rite, giving it time to make the insides of her cheeks creak in defence. Finally she let the liquid down into herself and contemplated her toothbrush routine. Today would be no joke.

Arriving at the grey slab of a building she loitered outside hoping for a voicemail or text message to divert her. It did not and she waited a little more just in case.

Through with the repetitive doings of the morning she had now become accustomed to, she found herself on the familiar varnished bench which was built for people shorter than her a long time ago.

She looked up and the defendant was in his place alongside the others, the well-fed defence and prosecution troubadours, the man in drag and the various families above, their faces hollowed out canoes, skin so thin that the water seeping in was almost visible.

Yesterday was an atomic icebreaker and now they were sitting amongst the slushy shards of realisation that would never truly evaporate. You only usually read about these things. Mouths moved and voices delivered but yesterday's pictures were on everyone's minds.

Pictures. Light reflected and refracted in order to convey images representing various moments in time. Various as in several, as in repetitive and continuous, as was suggested, as was inferred and ever so apparent.

At the recess, the point for discussion and the time for comfort breaks, the jury, silenced en masse, were pitifully absent of themselves. They had locked themselves away. Their cell contained several cheese plants, a large conference table with chairs, a tin of variety biscuits and flasks of tea and coffee. The light flickered occasionally as the traffic rolled past out through the window. Then a tweed man who held on to the bridge of his glasses suggested,

Let each person speak their mind, guilty or not.

The jury members nodded after each brief 'guilty'. One man, a fifty-year-old tub, reclined back in his chair and concentrated on spinning a plastic pen top as he nodded. A woman with long acrylic nails and a loud brooch fiddled with her fringe as if trying to release a small insect. A young man, no more than twenty five, clasped and unclasped, clasped and unclasped his wrist watch. Although there was unanimous agreement it seemed there was no desire to come to a conclusion. The jury members all looked to the floor as if concentrating on the carpet tiles could defer the necessity to move on with the day.

This sort of thing has been going on forever. She had thought she was of the generation who had words. We have processes and agencies and rehabilitation programmes and press coverage. We have crime squads and black lists and protests and petitions. We have hysteria and awareness and finger-pointing. We have recognition and rules and sentences.

Then, a small, willow-voiced man who had clearly lived through the lot, those wars we know about, the make-do-and-mend which is supposed to be fashionably resurfacing about now, said *I'd say hang him, but we can't.*

Sombrero Heights

Where a distance lies
over us
a parched sky swims
cloudless
and dizzy like
Sombrero Heights
in the summer

scarcely a word
between us flames
as others creep
into the backdrop

all over us
where a distance flies
dizzily in the cloudless sky
wheeling like sombreros,
a something waits
cactus-like
needling in the heat
as we walk towards the Heights.